D1581879

9112000029804

Capital Cities of the United Kingdom

London

Anita Ganeri and Chris Oxlade

raintree

a Capstone company — publishers for children

Raintree is an imprint of Capstone Global Library Limited, a company incorporated in England and Wales having its registered office at 264 Banbury Road, Oxford, OX2 7DY – Registered company number: 6695582

www.raintree.co.uk
myorders@raintree.co.uk

Edited by Helen Cox Cannons
Designed by Philippa Jenkins
Original illustrations © Capstone Global Library Ltd 2016
Picture research by Eric Gohl
Production by Victoria Fitzgerald
Originated by Capstone Global Library Ltd
Printed and bound in China

ISBN 978 1 4747 2766 2
20 19 18 17 16
10 9 8 7 6 5 4 3 2 1

British Library Cataloguing in Publication Data
A full catalogue record for this book is available from the British Library.

Acknowledgements
We would like to thank the following for permission to reproduce photographs: Capstone: Oxford Designer and Illustrators, cover (map), 1, 5; © Collins Bartholomew Ltd 2016. Reproduced with permission of HarperCollins Publishers: 28; Dreamstime: Anna Moskvina, 22, trentham, 25; Getty Images: Heritage Images, 6; iStockphoto: Anthony Brown, 10, southerlycourse, 13; Newscom/ZUMA Press: Alex Lentati, 21, Andrew Parsons, 27, Felipe Trueba, 20; Shutterstock: Bikeworldtravel, 26, Botond Horvath, 12, donsimon, 14, ileana_bt, 4, IR Stone, 15, 18, Kamira, 17, landmarkmedia, 16, mkos83, 11, peresanz, 8, photo.ua, 24, pio3, 23, QQ7, 9, Stuart Monk, cover, Tupungato, 19; Wikimedia: Eluveitie, 7.

Every effort has been made to contact copyright holders of material reproduced in this book. Any omissions will be rectified in subsequent printings if notice is given to the publisher.

All the internet addresses (URLs) given in this book were valid at the time of going to press. However, due to the dynamic nature of the internet, some addresses may have changed, or sites may have changed or ceased to exist since publication. While the author and publisher regret any inconvenience this may cause readers, no responsibility for any such changes can be accepted by either the author or the publisher.

Contents

Some words are shown in bold, **like this.**
You can find out what they mean by looking
in the glossary.

Where is London?

Every country has a capital city. The capital is the most important city in that country. London is the capital city of England. It is also the capital of the United Kingdom. The **Parliament** of the United Kingdom is in London.

Big Ben is the clocktower at the Houses of Parliament.

This is a map showing where London and England are in the British Isles.

SCOTLAND

NORTHERN IRELAND

REPUBLIC OF IRELAND

WALES

ENGLAND

London

Around 8.5 million people live in London. This makes it the biggest city in the whole of the United Kingdom. London lies on the River Thames in the south-east of England.

The story of London

The Romans **invaded** Britain nearly 2,000 years ago. They built a bridge over the River Thames. They also built a **fort** on the riverbank. The Romans called the city Londinium.

Londinium was the capital of Roman Britain. This is what it may have looked like in Roman times.

This **monument** stands where the Great Fire of London began.

In 1665, a terrible disease, called the Great **Plague**, struck London. It killed around 100,000 people. During the next year, in 1666, the Great Fire of London destroyed thousands of homes and buildings. The fire started in Pudding Lane.

London today

Today, London is a huge, busy city. Every day, around 3 million people travel into the city. People go there to work, go shopping, visit amazing museums and galleries, and admire the buildings.

This is the view from London's tallest building – the Shard.

This grand building is the home of the Bank of England.

London is one of the most important cities in the world for banking and business. It has many tall buildings called skyscrapers, filled with busy offices. The famous Bank of England opened in 1694.

The River Thames

The River Thames flows through London. The level of the water in the river rises and falls because of the **tide**. To the east of the city, the river is very wide and deep. There are **docks** where large ships load and unload.

Barges carry cargo along the River Thames.

The London Eye

This high-speed river bus is heading towards the London Eye.

The River Thames is important for transport. Boats, called river buses, carry passengers up and down the river. They pass many famous places, such as Tower Bridge and the London Eye.

Getting around London

Every day, millions of people travel in and out of London. The streets are busy with traffic, including the famous black taxicabs and red buses. Traffic crosses the River Thames on many beautiful bridges, and through road tunnels.

There are around 21,000 black cabs and 9,000 red double-decker buses in London.

Every day around 4 million people travel on the Tube.

The London Underground railway is known as the "Tube". This is because the tunnels are tube-shaped. The Underground has many different lines going in different directions. The Metropolitan Line was the world's first underground railway line. It opened in 1863.

London's buildings

The Tower of London is one of London's oldest buildings. It dates back to 1066. The Tower has been a royal palace and a prison. Guards at the Tower of London are called Yeoman Warders.

The Tower of London is home to the **crown jewels** of England.

Westminster Abbey has been the setting for every king or queen's **coronation** since the year 1066.

Westminster Abbey is a very famous church in the middle of London. Many kings and queens of England have been crowned there. In 2011, Prince William married Kate Middleton (now the Duchess of Cambridge) in Westminster Abbey.

Fun places

Madame Tussauds museum was opened in 1836 by a French **sculptor** called Madame Tussaud. It is packed with pop stars, sports stars and stars of film and television. None of them are real, though. They are all made of wax!

One Direction were first made into wax at Madame Tussauds in April 2013.

People come to the Globe theatre to see Shakespeare's plays, as they did 400 years ago.

William Shakespeare (1564–1616) was a very famous writer. He wrote plays and poems. His plays were performed in the Globe Theatre in London. The theatre burned down in 1613 but a new Globe was built in 1997.

Museums and galleries

London has many museums, packed with amazing objects. These include **animated** dinosaurs in the Natural History Museum and old spacecraft in the Science Museum. The British Museum is full of treasures from around the world, including Egyptian mummies.

A dinosaur skeleton stands in the entrance hall of the Natural History Museum.

This is one of the galleries inside the Tate Modern.

Tate Modern is one of London's most popular art galleries. It has thousands of works by modern artists. Tate Modern is beside the banks of the River Thames. You can cross the Millennium Bridge to reach it.

Hidden gems

Not far from the Houses of **Parliament** are the Churchill War Rooms. They are a maze of rooms and tunnels deep underground. During **World War II** Prime Minister Sir Winston Churchill (1874–1965) worked here. He had to stay safe from German bombing.

Winston Churchill slept in this bed in the War Rooms.

Visitors to the London Dungeon enjoy many scary things!

In the London Dungeon, you can find out about some of the capital's most bloodthirsty times. This includes the story of one of King Henry VIII's wives, Anne Boleyn. He had her head chopped off.

Shopping in London

Oxford Street is one of the busiest shopping streets in England. One of the most famous large shops there is Selfridges. The store opened in 1909 to great excitement. Thirty police officers had to hold back a large crowd of excited shoppers.

Shoppers come to see Oxford Street's Christmas Lights.

You can buy anything from fresh pizza to old books.

Camden Lock Market is a lively market, close to Regent's Canal. Stallholders sell crafts, books, clothes, **antiques** and lots more. It is a good place to look for a bargain.

Sport in London

Wembley Stadium is the biggest sports stadium in the United Kingdom. It has room for up to 90,000 people. Many important football matches, such as the FA Cup Final, are played here.

The England football team plays at Wembley Stadium.

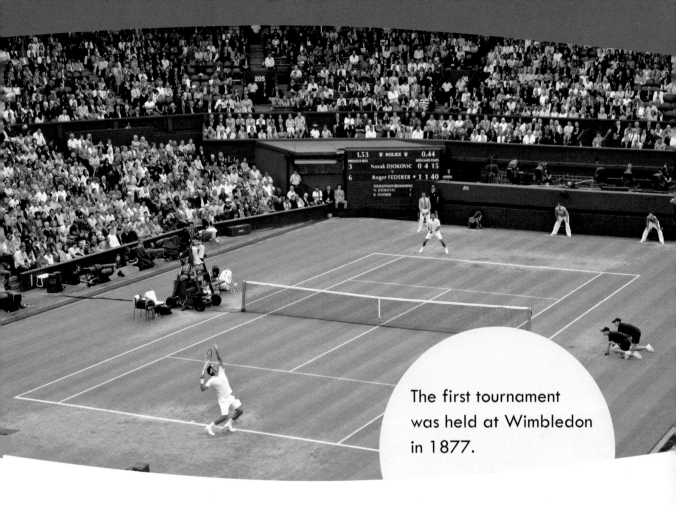

The first tournament was held at Wimbledon in 1877.

The All-England Lawn Tennis Club in Wimbledon is home to the world's most famous tennis **tournament.** Every July, the world's top players play there to try to become Wimbledon Champion. The matches are played on beautiful grass courts.

Festivals and celebrations

The Notting Hill Carnival is Europe's biggest street festival. It is held in August every year by Notting Hill's **Caribbean** community. Thousands of people dress up in colourful costumes and dance to music played by **steel bands**.

The Notting Hill Carnival parade is lively and noisy.

26

The Lord Mayor's carriage is on display in the Museum of London.

The Lord Mayor's Show is a parade of bands, decorated floats and soldiers on horseback. The Lord Mayor of London travels in a golden carriage, pulled by horses. Hundreds of thousands of people line the streets to watch.

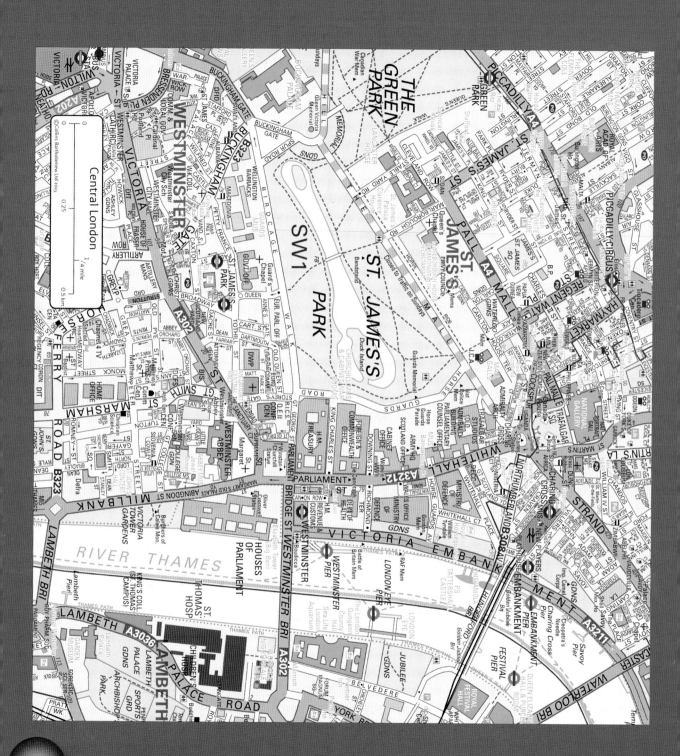

Glossary

animated made to move so that it looks alive

antique rare or valued object from the past

Caribbean coming from the Caribbean islands

coronation ceremony of crowning a king or queen

crown jewels crown and other jewellery worn by a king or queen

dock place where ships are built or where they are loaded and unloaded

fort building with strong walls that protects people inside from attack

invade send armed forces into another country to try to take it over

monument building or statue to celebrate a person or event

Parliament place where a country's laws are made

plague disease that causes fever and boils on the skin

sculptor type of artist who creates sculptures

steel band musical band that plays tunes by hitting steel drums

tide rise and fall of the sea at the coast

tournament sporting contest in which the winner is the person who wins the most games

World War II war fought by many of the world's countries between 1939 and 1945

29

Find out more

Books

Children's History of London, Jim Pipe (Hometown World, 2015)

London (Eyewitness Travel Guides) (Dorling Kindersley, 2015)

Things to Spot in London Sticker Book (Usborne Publishing, 2015)

Websites

lordmayorsshow.london
The official website of the Lord Mayor's Show, with information about the history of the parade and its famous mayors.

www.visitlondon.com
This is the official website of Visit London, with lots of information on sights to see, places to eat and events to go to.

www.visitlondon.com/discover-london/tower-bridge-webcam
A webcam that watches Tower Bridge across the Thames. You might even see the bridge opening and closing!

Places to visit

Places mentioned in the book
Shakespeare's Globe, 21 New Globe Walk, Bankside SE1 9DT
www.shakespearesglobe.com

The London Eye, Riverside Building, County Hall, Westminster Bridge Road SE1 7PB
www.londoneye.com

The Natural History Museum, Cromwell Road, London SW7 5BD
www.nhm.ac.uk

The Tower of London, London EC3N 4AB
www.hrp.org.uk/tower-of-london

More places to visit
Buckingham Palace, London SW1A 1AA
www.royal.gov.uk/theroyalresidences/buckinghampalace/buckinghampalace.aspx

London Zoo, Regent's Park, London NW1 4RY
www.zsl.org/zsl-london-zoo

Index